# Horrors, Terrors, Errors: A Poetry Chapbook

Ibrahim S. Amin

Published by Debonair Walrus, 2021.

While every precaution has been taken in the preparation of this book, the publisher assumes no responsibility for errors or omissions, or for damages resulting from the use of the information contained herein.

HORRORS, TERRORS, ERRORS: A POETRY CHAPBOOK

**First edition. October 31, 2021.**

Copyright © 2021 Ibrahim S. Amin.

ISBN: 979-8201698164

Written by Ibrahim S. Amin.

# Table of Contents

For Deej, whom I've roped into watching a lot of horror over
the years

# Introduction: Aristotle's Horrifics

Aristotle died in the 4th century BC, long before the rise of horror as a distinct genre. But he understood it anyway. That comes across in his *Poetics*, where he wrote about the catharsis audiences could obtain at the theatre. They'd watch horrible events unfold in a tragic play, experience fear and pity through the distance and filter of fiction, then leave the theatre and return to the real world, emotionally cleansed.

If you've ever had your heart race or spine tingle watching, reading, playing, or hearing horror, you can probably relate to that.

The poems in this book vary quite a lot (I've tried to arrange them loosely by horror sub-genre, beginning with the slasher poems), but whatever your tastes, you'll hopefully find something that'll deliver a dose of catharsis amidst the blood and gore.

# Sixteen Candles

Their voices grew with passing years,
At six they whispered, she ignored,
At ten they rasped inside her ears,
On sixteen's blazing cake, they roared.

She screamed and pledged to pay their price,
The long-awaited sacrifice,
She grasped the knife and offered death;
The flames ate blood instead of breath.

~~~~~

If you stop and think about it, the custom of birthday candles resembles an occult ritual, albeit with an edible altar. Form-wise, this one's a rispetto. Which seems fitting, because I typically associate Italian words with food (I contemplate cannoli more than anyone really should), and "rispetto" sounds like it could be a dessert.
~~~~~

# Slasher's True Love

She had risen to slaughter the boys at school,
For her grave had been shallow, her murder cruel,
And she scoured the buildings to seize a tool.

From the beer-glugging dorm, the first trudged to piss,
So she stalked to the toilets, her knife a kiss,
And she crimsoned his flow, but it brought no bliss.

To the roleplaying club she went wielding axe,
And D20s were scattered in gory whacks,
But no pleasure, catharsis, in those attacks.

In the cricket pavilion a batsman dressed,
Then he shrieked, and her chainsaw was splitting chest,
Yet she sighed, for his doom left her unimpressed.

But by chance, when he staggered, a hammer fell,
And its murderous clang was the reaper's knell,
And she snatched it and laughed with the wrath of hell.

In each hammering crack, in each breaking head,
In each splattering brain, in each howl of dread,
She was living in carnage, no longer dead.

Like the mythical heroes with magic steel,
Every slasher must bond with a weapon's feel,
In its signature slaughter, vengeance can heal.

~~~~~
~~~~~

Signature weapons are a great way of giving fictional characters a little extra flavour. The cartoons I watched as a kid in the '80s were full of such things, as were the decade's slasher movies. Sure, Freddy Kreuger, Jason Voorhees, and other horror movie killers would often use different weapons or killing methods to vary things up for the audience. But Freddy's finger-blade glove and Jason's machete have become iconic for a reason.

This poetic form's a stornello. And if the rispetto makes me think of desserts, I suppose a stornello would be something warm and savoury. Its rhyme scheme's simple enough, but I find its hendecasyllabic (eleven-syllable) lines a bit more complicated, since I feel they're too long to forgo metre altogether, but, with that being a prime number, they also won't divide perfectly. Hence you have to use a mixed metre of some kind. Here, I went with anapaests (di-di-dum) but then switched to an iamb (di-dum) at the end of each line. Like a jarring hammer blow.

# The Circle of Knife

Clowns kill kids,
Revenge-seeking,
Blood-dripping blades,
Laughing becomes screaming,
Savage minds make horrors,
Until...
Horrors make minds savage,
Screaming becomes laughing,
Blades dripping blood,
Seeking revenge,
Kids kill clowns.

<div align="center">~~~~~</div>

I'm a big believer in messing around with a variety of poetic forms, since each offers a different kind of puzzle to solve, and they make you ponder words in different ways. That's certainly true of palindromes, or mirror poems. You have a bridge word ("until", in this case), and after that you repeat the previous words of the poem, but in reverse order. Simple concept, but it brings a lot of challenges when you try it out.

# Prey That Cools

Stalk the streets
Stalk your prey
Prey that runs
Prey that screams
Screams of fear
Screams of pain
Pain you bring
Pain you drink
Drink the shadows
Drink the moonlight
Moonlight shines
Moonlight knows
Knows your crimes
Knows your heart
Heart and horror
Heart and blade
Blade you bought
Blade you love
Love the dark
Love the chase
Chase your victim
Chase your dreams
Dreams of night
Dreams of life
Life is short
Life is sweet
Sweet sorrows
Sweet shimmers
Shimmers on puddles
Shimmers of neon

Neon signs
Neon streets
Streets that glow
Streets that twist
Twist and tangle
Twist and turn
Turn to darkness
Turn the corner
Corner your prey
Corner your pleasure
Pleasure and pain
Pleasure and puddles
Puddles of moonlight
Puddles of blood
Blood warms
Blood cools
Cools the chase
Cools your soul
Soul...
Chase...

<center>~~~~~</center>

Robert Keim invented this form, the blitz, and it's both fun and fast to write. I don't think I've ever written a 50-line poem so quickly before. As you can see, the pairs of short phrases begin with the same starting word, and the last word in each pair becomes the starting word of the next pair, for the first 48 lines. No punctuation. After that, you reuse the final words of lines 48 and 47, in that order, and those become lines 49 and 50. The title of a blitz poem follows a formula too. You take the first words of lines 3 and 47 (again, in that order), and put a conjunction or preposition between them.

In my head, this kind of poem sounds a bit like the "choose life" monologue from the movie *Trainspotting*.

11

# Threes

Three blades flashed,
Three throats slashed,
Three lives splashed.

Three graves dug,
Three dead lugged,
Three holes plugged.

Three come back,
Three attack,
Three skulls crack.

~~~~~

This one's a tricube, a form Phillip Larrea invented. The rules are very simple: three stanzas, three lines in each stanza, three syllables in each line. I went with a rhyme scheme and used the same starting word for each line, but those aren't requirements of the form.
~~~~~

# The Hatchet Man

The Hatchet Man comes,
His stalking step drums,
He cleaves;
He hunts in the slums,
The rich city's crumbs,
He reaves;
His hatchet blade thrums,
His trophies, their thumbs,
He leaves.

~~~~~

Whichever French poet first invented this nine-line form, the lai, they probably didn't imagine it framing the exploits of a hatchet-wielding maniac. But I love how a lai's two-syllable b-rhyme lines can become hatchet hacks between the five-syllable a-rhyme couplets.
~~~~~

# Carrion Cats

In bygone days, the beasts, they knew
To gather when the fighters hew,
The wolves and ravens saw
The weapons warlike humans wield
And followed, thinking, "Battlefield!
We'll eat our fill of gore!"

The modern feline knows as well:
"The slashers' blades send teens to hell,
So Halloween's our treat!"
The masked marauders hack and stab,
Meowing cats emerge and grab
Their share of tasty meat.

~~~~~

Tom Holland (the historian, not the actor) made me aware of the theory that medieval wolves and ravens got so used to feasting after battles, they began following armies around, knowing the sight of so many armed humans meant another such feast was coming. Kind of like when cats hear you crinkle a packet of treats. Or in this case, when slashers prowl and kill.

The form's another French one, a rime couee.
~~~~~

# Inked

This shop was never here before,
The whisky blurred his eyes and brain,
He'd drunk too much, but he was sure.

"My needle causes little pain!"
The smiling tattoo artist winked,
"I've never had a lad complain!"

Outside the shop, the raindrops plinked,
"I came here wanting vindaloo..."
"That bloke owed money, off he slinked."

"I rent here now, so come on through,
We ladies love a man with tats!"
He shrugged; he'd nothing else to do.

He browsed the pictures, skulls and cats,
A dagger, bloody, runes and charms,
And grinning, pointed: "Vampire bats!"

She made him sit and inked his arms,
He squinted, had that bat just flapped?
"I'm drunk as fuck! Just false alarms..."

He paid, she smirked, and thunder clapped,
He stumbled home, he slumped and woke;
His bats had vanished while he napped!

"The fuck's this shit? Some kind of joke!?!

That scamming bitch just used a pen!
I'll get my cash or sue her broke!"

He stormed the streets, and marvelled then;
The smell of spices hit his nose;
"You want the vindaloo again?"

"The curry house? You didn't close!?!"
The chef said, "Mate, you feeling fine?"
A dozen other "Fucks!" arose.

He wandered round, but found no sign;
He told his wife but she just laughed,
"You must've dreamed it, drunk as swine!"

He checked his wallet, feeling daft,
And every single note was there;
"Next time, I'll fucking stick to draught."

His new assistant's auburn hair
Soon burned such follies from his mind;
A business trip, his next affair.

He coaxed the girl, they wined and dined,
He wallowed smug in victory,
Till morning, when the mirror shined.

"That tattoo artist's fucked with me!"
His forearm bore his conquest's name,
His skin was maledictory!

Impossible! His mind aflame,
His wife would see and slap his face!
What explanation could he claim?

He wrapped a bandage round the place,
He'd have it lasered, seared away!
His wife would never see a trace!

The bandage kept her name at bay,
He held his nerve, but then it cracked,
The ink had spread, a new display.

Affairs with girls whose names he lacked,
Pornography now filled his chest,
Including crimes, each groping act.

He grabbed his shirt to hide the rest,
But spurting cocks defiled his brow,
His breaking brain decried the jest.

He'd save himself! Despairing now,
He grabbed some scissors, carved for gore,
He'd flay the guilt away, somehow!

They heard his screams and broke the door,
And found him, skinless, on the floor.

~~~~~

A friend of mine, Rhynn, retrained as a tattoo artist a few years back
(they were originally a videogame artist, which is how we met, working
together in that industry). Since then, they've constantly amazed me
~~~~~

with the dark magic of the designs they inscribe on people's flesh. That inspired this poem. If you want to see their work for yourself, their Instagram handle is @nnyhr.

The form here is an Italian one, terza rima. It's what Dante used in his *Divine Comedy*, another tale involving supernatural punishment.

# Midnight Rider

The Midnight Rider's demon gleams in black,
Her engine howls his ancient blasphemies
That shattered heaven's hosts on hell's attack,
Before that angel cleaved his wrists and knees
And hurled him down, impaled upon the trees;
The Midnight Rider laughs behind her wheel,
And aims the demon's living ebon steel,
She yearns for speed and racing glory days,
The demon yearns for blood and made a deal,
She runs them down, he drinks the crimson haze.

~~~~~


Another French form (a dizain), and another poem inspired by a friend's exploits. Niki races, and is always looking for ways to tear around each track faster and faster, pursuing speed and glory. If she could fashion a racing vehicle from a demon's body, I'm sure she would.
~~~~~

# Whitest Stag

The whitest stag once held the door
Its flesh the wall, its blood the key
The laughing goddess walks once more

She giggled mankind's fatal flaw
Her cackles shredded sanity
The whitest stag once held the door

A hundred cities drowned in gore
She chuckled their depravity
The laughing goddess walks once more

"Invoking heaven's ancient law
I, Queen of Gods, imprison thee!"
The whitest stag once held the door

But greedy mortals grasp and claw
"That whitest hide, a prize for me!"
The laughing goddess walks once more

Its life was ice, its blood the thaw
Its prison broken, captive free
The whitest stag once held the door
The laughing goddess walks once more

~~~~~


Towards the end of September 2021, a white deer strayed into the town
of Bootle and ran around the place, until the police killed it in the
~~~~~

name of public safety (wildlife experts had asked them to leave it alone instead). Social media was full of jokes about how it all sounded like an ill-omen from a fairytale. Hence this villanelle.

26

# Infestation

She grinds her heel upon a hive
These things infest her lost domain
Her kingdom gone, but they survive?
She grinds her heel upon a hive
Her slumber let their cities thrive
The elder goddess ends their reign
She grinds her heel upon a hive
These things infest her lost domain

~~~~~

The triolet's a very economical type of poem, with so much repetition among its eight lines (the first line appearing three times gives the form its name). As with the previous villanelle, I think ominous repetition lends itself well to cosmic horror and the destruction wrought by angry or callous elder gods.
~~~~~

# Home

The ancient city calls me home,
I glimpse it when I sleep,
It gleamed before the rise of Rome,
It drowned beneath the deep.

The seething seas disgorged its might,
The oceans choked and failed,
Its eldritch power won the fight,
They frothed, and groaned, and wailed.

Forgotten temples echo songs,
A language lost to time,
The chanting tongues of long-dead throngs,
They gibber, claw, and rhyme.

My friend has fallen far behind,
The madness gnawed his brain,
He tore his eyes and howled there, blind,
A bullet took his pain.

The cyclopean idol calls,
I walk an empty street,
The city's ancient darkness falls,
Beneath its shroud we'll meet.

~~~~~

I tried to give this poem a bit of a Lovecraftian vibe, and even used one of H. P. Lovecraft's favourite words ("cyclopean").
~~~~~

Although it doesn't really fit the tone I'm going for here, there's a fun quirk with this particular metre (alternating iambic tetrameters and trimeters): Any poem you write in it can be sung to the tune of *Yellow Rose of Texas*, or the theme song from *Pokemon*. Emily Dickinson used it extensively, and her poems hit very differently when you sing them to the *Pokemon* music.

# The Cultist's Prayer

Our dark messiah, rise at last!
Your dreaded day is now at hand!
This age of mortal man has passed!

O son of fallen father, stand!
The victims drench your altar's stones!
Your dreaded day is now at hand!

We splash their brains and break their bones!
We've raised an army draped in sin!
The victims drench your altar's stones!

Destroy his angels, lead the djinn!
The Nazarene in heaven bawls!
We've raised an army draped in sin!

We'll burn the Kaaba, smash St. Paul's!
The world shall blaze where we have trod!
The Nazarene in heaven bawls!

Your tentacles shall choke their god!
The world shall blaze where we have trod!
Our dark messiah, rise at last!
This age of mortal man has passed!

~~~~~

Earlier, we had a terza rima (*Inked*) and a villanelle (*Whitest Stag*). Lewis
Turco combined elements of those two forms to create this one, the
~~~~~

terzanelle, and its pattern of refrains (repeated lines) seemed to fit a prayer or chant.

# Chimera

She stitched her beast from different parts:
The banshee's head to shriek its cry,
The werewolf's torso, fearsome claws,
The writhing tentacles below.

The banshee's head to shriek its cry,
Announcing that her foes would die,
They'd know she'd slain them, and know why.

The werewolf's torso, fearsome claws,
To splinter through the strongest doors,
And strew their innards, drench the floors.

The writhing tentacles below,
They'd slither where no steps could go,
Leave slimy emerald trails aglow.

~~~~~

Charles A. Stone invented the trimeric. This form doesn't require a metre or rhyme scheme, only that the second, third, and fourth lines of the opening quatrain (four-line stanza) become the first lines of the subsequent tercets (three-line stanzas), in order. I thought leaving the quatrain unrhymed but including a rhyme to bind each tercet might suit the image of a monster that's stitched together from separate parts.
~~~~~

# Terrors of the Tenement

The gargoyle perches, crunching snacks,
Revenge for pigeons' shit attacks,
He rents the roof by standing guard,
The burglars soar and plummet hard.
A banshee rents the top-floor flat,
She tells a funny tale of that:
The prior tenant, doomed for sin,
She shrieked his omen, moved right in.
The vampire downstairs games at night,
He paints his windows, shuns the light,
And when the banshee screams this late,
He wonders, "Doom? Or just a date?"
The mummy misses Egypt's sand,
Jihadists drove him from that land,
Declaring, "Undead anger God!"
"I've never even met that sod..."
A human rents the ground-floor place,
And keeps the terror from her face,
"Respect their cultures!" tells herself,
But keeps a sword upon her shelf.
The basement ghoul is seldom seen,
His diet keeps the building clean,
He drags their victims down his stairs,
And leaves no bones or even hairs.

~~~~~

Since this one depicts a tenement or apartment block and its denizens, it seemed fitting to leave the lines unbroken in a single stanza, to create a matching visual.
~~~~~

# Golden Gravediggers

Once, before the hungry dead came back,
Upon the dirt we'd tossed them into,
A gravedigger's job soothed the soul, with the
Midnight moon that makes Earth her chamber,
Dreary but never stomach-turning,
While the world slumbered, I buried them all;
I long for such tranquil times, oh my,
Pondered them with all my yearning soul;
Weak, you think me? No strength left within?
And yet they sent you here to help me;
Weary work... Those groans? Zombies, burning.

~~~~~

Terrance Hayes invented a type of poem called the golden shovel. You write one by taking a line from another poet's poem, and making each of its words (in the same order) the end words of your own lines, meaning anyone who reads downwards at the edge of your poem can read the other poet's original line. I decided to double-up on that. If you read down both edges of this poem, you'll find two different lines from Edgar Allan Poe's *The Raven*. And since we have those two golden shovels working alongside each other, I call this form golden gravediggers.
~~~~~

# Riders of the Cruel Caliph

They say he broke a rule,
The riders serve the Cruel Caliph,
They name the boy a thief;
"This village lacks belief in God!"
A rider wields the rod,
And taunts the priestess plodding near:
"I'll teach kuffar to sneer
At Allah's law, now hear him shriek!"
"I know you riders seek
To break our will, you're speaking lies,
You want our gods' demise,
To snatch our idols' eyes of gold,
And smash the shrines we hold,
Your Cruel Caliph has told you, 'Ride!
Harass them, strip their pride,
Convert kuffar, deride their ways!'"
"You bitch!" a rider says,
He knocks her down and slays the child,
"I'll see your gods defiled!
I'll order corpses piled up high,
Your shrine a feast for fly and crow!"
He strikes another blow;
The priestess claws the flowing blood,
She smears its crimson flood,
And carves her curse in mud and gore,
Invoking ancient law;
Then later, palace, glory's due,
The evening deepens blue,
The riders, boasting through their feast,
Now growl with voice of beast,

And, somewhere far, the priestess grins,
In fur they wear their sins,
Their werewolf rage brings instant doom,
The bloody splashes bloom,
The crescent moon's a looming blade
Above the bodies, splayed,
And through the palace, wading red,
They hunt the man who's fled,
The Cruel Caliph, his head the prize,
For idols' golden eyes.

~~~~~

The luc bat's a Vietnamese form, and works a bit like a rhyming relay race. You have alternating six and eight-syllable lines, with each eight-syllable line taking the end-rhyme of the previous six-syllable line on its own sixth syllable, then handing off a fresh rhyme from its eighth syllable, which becomes the end-rhyme of the following six-syllable line.

I went with a crescent moon rather than the traditional full moon because of the Islamic symbolism, which pagan gods might enjoy mocking in their lycanthropic curse. And if it worked with both orientations of the crescent, you'd end up with twice as many werewolf attacks each lunar month.
~~~~~

# The Vampire Drinks

The vampire drinks the blood of kings,
Amasses wealth his long life brings,
He savours throats his fangs have burst,
And golden goblets quench his thirst,
Reclining while fair Sappho sings.

His palace falls, marauders' slings,
For centuries the loss still stings,
Medieval plague-tinged blood is cursed;
The vampire drinks.

The sound of breaking bottles rings,
A tearing backpack holds his things,
He sleeps in alleys, fate reversed,
This smacked-up junkie blood's the worst,
Eternal life's shit, yet he clings;
The vampire drinks.

~~~~~

Vampire fiction's a great place to explore the consequences of immortality, whether good or bad, and I think the repeated partial line you get in a rondeau helps convey the sense of eternal decline and misery.
~~~~~

# Jessica Jekyll & Harriet Hyde

Transylvanian downpour had slathered her face,
But then Jessica Jekyll had spotted the place,
The hotel she was booked at, she'd sighed in relief,
But now, dripping its lobby, she gasped disbelief
As she sloughed off the water that drenched her and chilled,
For ahead was a woman of amazon build.
"Oh no!" Jessica groaned, and the woman, she whirled
And she grabbed for a suitcase and heaved it and hurled,
And when Jessica dodged and it crashed on the floor,
The receptionist cried, "Let's not have any more
Of this murderous violence; the Count will be pissed!
This convention has rules, so, good lady, desist!"
"Ha! No lady," said Jessica, "Harriet Hyde!
I was hoping the rumours were true that you'd died!
What the hell is a Hyde, common thug, doing here?
Did you blunder inside with a head full of beer?"
"Common thug? I'm the queen of the nutters, the peak!
But if Jessica Jekyll must stick in her beak,
I'm invited, a guest, and a flash VIP!"
And she whipped out a pass and said, "Look at it! See?"
"It's a joke, or a prank; you're unworthy of this!"
The receptionist coughed, "Are you checking in, miss?"
But ignoring her, Jessica cried: "Just one hitch...
This convention's for brains; where's your doctorate, bitch?"
"A degree's just a scrap fit for wrapping my chips!"
"And you've eaten too many, to judge by those hips..."
"It's my blood, and my genes, and they've brought me to show
That you Jekylls are twats, and I'm striking a blow
For us Hydes; since they split us, our bloodline's the best!
We got muscles and mayhem, I call myself blessed!"

"Ha! Oh, Harriet, dear, all you Hydes are a curse!"
The receptionist winced, "I'm afraid this gets worse...
See, we've run out of rooms, and you're having to share!"
And one woman protested, one roared like a bear,
But the vampire who managed the place couldn't budge,
And so Jessica, Harriet, forced then to trudge
Up the stairs, to their room, had one final surprise,
For the room had a bed, and no twin met their eyes.
"No! No! Harriet, sleep on the sofa or floor!"
"Huh? No, Jessica, fuck you, and fuck you once more!"
And the women both glared, but when neither backed down,
At last, Jessica shrugged and declared with a frown,
"So we'll share, just don't slaughter the maid in the bath,
Like you Hydes do whenever you give in to wrath!"
But then Harriet gobbled some crisps in the bed,
And the open-mouthed crunch went to Jessica's head.
"Gah! I'm taking a walk! I don't care if it's cold!
And you'll clean up the crumbs—" "I don't do what I'm told,
I'm a Hyde, not a dog— " "So stop eating like one!"
And then Jessica stormed out, her patience was done,
And she wandered the streets and she came to a pub,
Of the sort where the tables get seldom a rub
From a cloth, and they stick to your elbows and glass,
But her mood was so bitter, she lowered her arse
On a stool at the bar and she ordered a drink,
"Is there something that's fruity? A cocktail that's pink?"
But the bartender grunted and slapped down an ale,
And yet Jessica paid him, and told him the tale
Of the Jekylls and Hydes, and their ancestor fool,
And a drinker who heard her said, "Why not play pool?"
Transylvanian hustlers had gathered, you see,
The convention had marks by the dozen or three,

And the scientist crowd? Just the prey that they sought,
But poor Jessica blundered, she hadn't been taught
In her books or her lab that the world's full of sharks,
And she played several games, merely thinking them larks,
Till the hustler said, "Girl, it is time to pay out!"
"Uh..." And checking her purse, she said, "Shit! I've got nowt..."
"You're a Jekyll! You'll give me your secrets to sell!"
And he pulled out a knife, "Or I'll send you to hell!"
But a woman said, "Dickhead! You wanted a taste
Of our ancestor's secrets? I'll lay you to waste!"
And then Harriet slapped the man, yielding a whine,
And she heaved him up high and she shattered his spine,
And she tore up the pub, left the tables in shards,
And she battered the drinkers and littered the yards,
And she flipped a police car that answered the call,
And demolished the pub, for she'd none left to brawl;
Down the street, past the wreckage and corpses and flame,
The two found a kebab house, 'The Slaughter' its name,
In there, Harriet ordered a feast and she munched,
And the bones in her chicken wings splintered and crunched.
"So," said Jessica, "Harriet, thanks for the save,
Transylvania's vicious, and nearly my grave!
But that carnage? Excessive! The murders? Too far!"
This left Harriet silent and scratching a scar.
They returned to their room and they lay in the bed,
And at last, in the darkness, "Yeah..." Harriet said,
"You're too simpering soft, and I'm murderous force."
"But I have a solution! The potion! Of course!"
In the morning they woke in a snuggle and dressed,
And then Harriet conquered and Jess did the rest;
First they annexed a lab, then they brewed up the drink,
Then they toasted with vials, and savoured the clink,

And for Jessica Jekyll, it strengthened her grit,
Whereas Harriet Hyde had it bolster her wit,
For those past science follies reverted to norm,
And together they took the convention by storm.

~~~~~

Some of my writing buddies have a deep love for the romance genre's bed-sharing trope, where characters who aren't in a romantic or sexual relationship, and may even despise each other, end up having to unexpectedly share a bed. A few of them were discussing it one night, while I was trying to think up the subject for my next horror poem. So I ran with it.
~~~~~

# Phantoms

Phantoms,
Roaming souls,
In the graveyard's dark,
May their eyes never find you,
Else your soul will scream forever in their ranks.

~~~~~

I call this form the Optimus Prime. The first letters of the lines spell "PRIME", and their syllable count ascends through the prime numbers (2, 3, 5, 7, 11).
~~~~~

# The Whispering Waves

They draw him to the edge of the world,
The witnessing, whispering waves,
They rise from glistening dark,
Foaming ghosts of that day
When his anger burned;
Their whispers chill,
He treads air,
The waves
Feed.

<div align="center">~~~~~</div>

A nonet entails beginning with a nine-syllable line, then having one fewer syllable each line, till you end the poem with a single syllable. I thought it might provide a good shape for a poem involving a person going over the edge of a cliff.

# The Places of Her Life

She roams the places of her life,
The mosque; she knelt and read Quran,
A molvi's slaps would blur her eyes
And make the carpet's patterns dance.

The schoolyard sleeps in silver glow;
She roams the places of her life,
Behind the shed where she'd unfurl
In dress and boots, and tossed hijab.

She shivers near the alley's mouth,
The place they took her when they learned;
She roams the places of her life,
The broken glass here glints like blades.

She watches girls who fear her fate,
And whispers words that help them live,
They don't get caught, they think that's luck;
She roams the places of her life.

~~~~~

A molvi teaches children to sound out Arabic for Quran recitation purposes (we didn't learn how to translate and understand it, just how to say it out loud). They're notoriously brutal men. If you mispronounced a word, they'd hit you. For most of us, especially boys, that sort of fundamentalist cruelty was thankfully as bad as it got. But others suffered far more. In fundamentalist families, girls who wanted to remove the hijab and wear western clothes, and enjoy the things other
~~~~~

children took for granted, had to do so in secret. If they got caught, their parents might beat them. Or worse.

The form here is a quatern, distinguished by the refrain, where the opening line repeats one line further down in each subsequent stanza.

# Halloween Menu

Night-Terror Terrine (on toast)
Roast Werewolf Ribs (in white wine)
Tentacles (fresh from the coast!)
Host-Flesh and Slivers of Spine

Madman Maghaz (spice and brain)
Pain-Drenched Ice Cream Dark Delight
Low-Tip Skewers (shanked in lane)
Slain Reviewers (torched tonight)

~~~~~

Irish forms of poetry are notoriously complicated. They have so many rules, you feel like a character in a folktale, trying to win a leprechaun's gold by writing him the poem he's asked for, only to have him add a new rule each time you show him what you've written. This rannaigheact mhor is only eight lines long, but it took me longer to write than any other poem in the book. In addition to the number of syllables per line and the alternating end-rhymes in each quatrain, the form also demands various numbers and placements of alliteration and cross-rhymes. And the poem has to end with the same sound it begins.

The menu format made it a bit easier than trying to weave a narrative under those conditions.

Oh, if you happen to see "maghaz" on the menu at a desi restaurant or takeaway, that really is a brain curry. Though the brain typically comes from a sheep rather than a madman.
~~~~~

# Strange Charcuterie

So beauty's deep as skin, they bleat?
A lie! It lives inside the meat!
My pork is long and quite the treat...

Just try the boneless toes with fries,
Those ballet dancers tenderise
Themselves and call it exercise,
You'll feel their rhythms while you eat!

A fighter's biceps, full of rage,
Testosterone with hint of sage,
You'll want to brawl inside a cage!
Serve with rice or bulgur wheat.

A politician's twisted tongue,
It's rich from every lie he flung,
And spiced by every voter stung,
It's food for brains to help you cheat.

A gamer's eyes have seen it all,
The battles, bloodshed, mankind's fall,
Each, fried, a crunchy flavour ball,
And seasoned from the games they beat.

An adult party? Why not cock?
Don't redden, giggle, gasp, or mock!
Encase it, bake a pastry sock,
A wanker's roll, it brings the heat.

~~~~~

One of my writing buddies, Stacey L. Polishook, writes dystopian cannibalism novels. Beta-reading for her always makes me crave red meat... Anyway, it seemed appropriate to offer her and everyone else a few serving suggestions.

The form's a zejel, which emerged from Islamic Spain and is characterised by its rhyme scheme in which the end-rhyme from the opening tercet returns in the last line of the following quatrains, after their previous lines have shared a different end-rhyme (aaa, bbba, ccca...).
~~~~~

# Her Gallery

Alas, the gallery will shortly close,
Your visit comes a little near the morn,
Nocturnal hours, thus our mistress chose,
She walks the night and curses rosy dawn,
Her favoured patrons savour times of gloom,
Besides which, sunlight's brightness spoils the art,
Chiaroscuro! Shadows shape the room,
The moon and stars do play a vital part;
Another night! Our guides have shuffled home,
Perhaps tomorrow, after sunlight dies...
A traveller? With just one night to roam?
I can't abide the sorrow in your eyes!
I'll guide you round and show you what I may,
Before the dark succumbs at last to day.


## The Sinless Harem

Before the dark succumbs at last to day,
Behold the sultan painted long ago,
He built the finest harem, where he'd play,
And stationed dogs so Allah wouldn't know;
Islamic lore declares two angels slog
Behind us, writing down each sin we make,
But angels cannot venture near a dog,
A loophole! Heaven made a grand mistake!
The angels bristled, thwarted, past his gate,
But harem women offered grim accord,
They cleaved the sultan's neck and sealed his fate,
A sinless murder! Heaven their reward!

One hungry hound here eats the sultan's thigh,
The women sport with houris, dance the sky.

**Ani's Burning Brand**

The women sport with houris, dance the sky,
But come, for other wonders wait at hand,
This heroine has raised her battle cry,
In orange blazes Ani's burning brand;
She'd dragged a drunk from flames and saved his hide,
The village mocked him, thus he wove a tale:
"That Ani walked through fire! She's Satan's bride!
Let's hang the bitch and make her dark lord wail!"
They placed the noose around her neck and cheered,
But Satan laughed and burned the rope away;
"You called her mine? I'll play along!" he jeered,
"And grant her hellfire; Ani, go and slay!"
Infernos burn, horizon glows like hearth;
Our mistress loves displays of female wrath!

**Death by Chocolate**

Our mistress loves displays of female wrath!
But finds amusement, giggles those who fall;
Not squeamish? See the painted gory bath,
But please don't paint your dinner 'pon the wall!
Elaine's romantic efforts yielded nought
But dates with wretched men who brought no thrill,
A valentine to give herself, she sought,
And paid a goddess blood to help her kill!
"A voraphile?" The goddess arched her brow,
"I'll make those menfolk chocolates, fill a box,

But heed this warning, mortal, 'fore you chow:
The spell will fade the moment midnight knocks!"
"I'll scoff them swiftly, done before it fails!"
The chewed-up corpses burst Elaine's entrails!

## The Shining Hero

The chewed-up corpses burst Elaine's entrails!
Assumptions break and slay the fools who wish
But seldom stop to think what such entails;
This sculpted, muscled hero, quite the dish...
He freed a djinn who offered great reward:
"Declare your wishes; three I'll bring to pass!"
"Heroic figure! Endless youth!" he cawed,
"And gorgeous women long to touch my arse!"
He's stood in castles, felt the hands of queens,
A famous actress groped his groin and sighed,
Their favourite places marked in metal's sheens,
They bear eternal witness, shining pride!
A wish begins a reckless test of fate,
The consequence reveals itself too late!

## Dress of Souls

The consequence reveals itself too late!
And tempus flees our gallery as well!
The dawn and thrice-damned sunlight soon await,
Be swift! Another painted tale I'll tell...
This princess wears a dress of captured souls,
She twirls among her mirrors, treads their shrieks,
Its fabric grants the power she controls,
Yet hungers, thus the finest souls she seeks,

The murderer and monster, fiend and lord,
Her dress can wield their darkness, make it hers,
But even brightest souls can swell its hoard,
Besides, in most the good and evil blurs...
She stalks the night and curses rosy dawn,
She seethes when hunger plagues her near the morn.

She seethes when hunger plagues her near the morn;
But quicker now, the greatest piece, ahead,
You'll feast your eyes before the night is torn,
It lies beyond these monsters' marble dread,
And Greek marauders painted sacking Troy;
Left, tentacled gods rise from frothing seas,
Right, butchery and bloodshed bring girls joy;
The final chamber's secrets outstrip these!
My key... Unlocked! My friend, do enter first,
Your soul has drunk the horrors seen tonight,
That flavour might appeal and quench her thirst;
You'll suffer only anguish if you fight!
I'd find a different victim, heaven knows,
Alas, the gallery will shortly close.

<div align="center">~~~~~</div>

If you watch a lot of horror, you've probably come across the horror
anthology format, movies or TV shows where some kind of framing
device surrounds the telling of separate stories. I tried to capture that
flavour via a crown of sonnets.

The theological quirk mentioned in *The Sinless Harem* is a real thing.
According to popular Islamic belief, two angels follow each of us around.
One records our good deeds. The other, bad deeds. For some reason,

Allah outsources those jobs to them, despite supposedly being omniscient and omnipresent. Which seems very lazy. Anyway, there's another Islamic belief, one of the various anti-dog teachings found in the Hadith. It claims angels won't enter a house that has a dog. That's seen as a bad thing, since you're supposed to want angels around, but in theory it also creates the loophole depicted in the sonnet. If the bad-deeds angel can't get in, you can sin away and he won't know. The perfect crime.

Ani from the second story was inspired by another of my writing buddies. The real Ani's surname is "Brandt", and she trained to rescue people from burning buildings and other disasters (she also trained dogs to locate survivors). Hence *Ani's Burning Brand* came to mind.

# Thanks to...

The great thing about poems, from an author's point of view, is they're short enough to inflict on everyone you know, via social media or whatever messaging apps you use to keep in touch. As a consequence, I have a number of long-suffering beta-readers I need to thank: Lena Gkika, Stacey L. Polishook, Airy Manning, Niki Pladson, Deej Amin, Kathleen Trembath, Ani Brandt, and Rhynn.

And thank you to my fellow WIPpersnappers. Writing's a lot more fun when you have a bunch of fellow writers with whom you can knock around ideas, or else just rant about stuff.

# About the Author

Ibrahim S. Amin was educated at the Manchester Grammar School, the University of Newcastle, and the University of Manchester. He wallowed in education for as long as he could, earning his PhD in Classics & Ancient History. At that point he ran out of excuses and joined the real world — where he now writes to support his unhealthy takeaway addiction.

His previous books are:

*The Monster Hunter's Handbook: The Ultimate Guide to Saving Mankind from Vampires, Zombies, Hellhounds, and Other Mythical Beasts* (published in Italian as *I Fratelli del Vampiro*)

*Jihad Squad*

*Clara Mandrake's Monster*

*Gorgon Street Girls*

*Apostasy, Blasphemy, Absurdity: A Poetry Chapbook*

*Fantasy, Fairies, Franiards: A Poetry Chapbook*

You can learn more about them, ask him questions, and read random musings on his Goodreads author page, or endure his rants on Twitter (@Ibrahim_S_Amin).

www.ingramcontent.com/pod-product-compliance
Lightning Source LLC
Chambersburg PA
CBHW031419160726

47993CB00003B/1310